HAL•LEONARD

JAZZ PLAY-ALONG®

Book and CD for B♭, E♭, C and Bass Clef Instruments

volume 88

Arranged and Produced by Mark Taylor

DUKE ELLINGTON
Favorites
10 Jazz Classics

Cover photo: Photofest

ISBN 978-1-4234-5473-1

HAL•LEONARD®
CORPORATION

7777 W. BLUEMOUND RD. P.O. BOX 13819 MILWAUKEE, WI 53213

Visit Hal Leonard Online at
www.halleonard.com

Duke Ellington Favorites

Volume 88

Arranged and Produced by
Mark Taylor

Featured Players:

Graham Breedlove–Trumpet
John Desalme–Tenor Saxophone
Tony Nalker–Piano
Jim Roberts–Bass
Leonard Cuddy–Drums

Recorded at Bias Studios, Springfield, Virginia
Bob Dawson, Engineer

HOW TO USE THE CD:

Each song has <u>two</u> tracks:

1) Split Track/Melody

Woodwind, Brass, Keyboard, and **Mallet Players** can use this track as a learning tool for melody style and inflection.

Bass Players can learn and perform with this track – Remove the recorded bass track by turning down the volume on the LEFT channel.

Keyboard and **Guitar Players** can learn and perform with this track – remove the recorded piano part by turning down the volume on the RIGHT channel.

2) Full Stereo Track

Soloists or **Groups** can learn and perform with this accompaniment track with the RHYTHM SECTION only.

CD

① : SPLIT TRACK/MELODY
② : FULL STEREO TRACK

CHELSEA BRIDGE

BY BILLY STRAYHORN

C VERSION

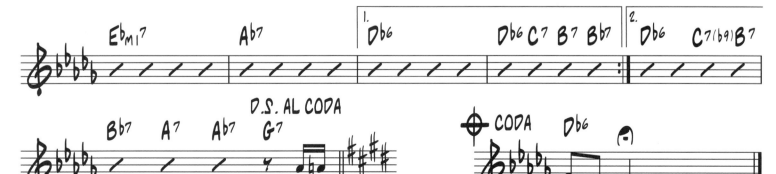

THE CREOLE LOVE CALL

BY DUKE ELLINGTON

CD
- ◆**3** : SPLIT TRACK/MELODY
- ◆**4** : FULL STEREO TRACK

C VERSION

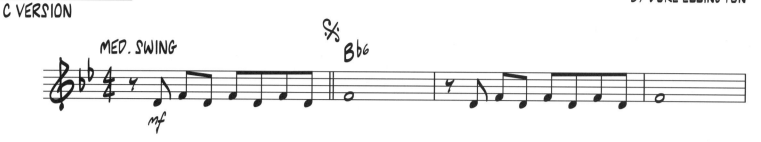

DANCERS IN LOVE

BY Duke Ellington

DAY DREAM

BY DUKE ELLINGTON AND
BILLY STRAYHORN

DROP ME OFF IN HARLEM

WORDS BY NICK KENNY
MUSIC BY DUKE ELLINGTON

CD

11 : SPLIT TRACK/MELODY
12 : FULL STEREO TRACK

EVERYTHING BUT YOU

BY DUKE ELLINGTON,
HARRY JAMES AND DON GEORGE

C VERSION

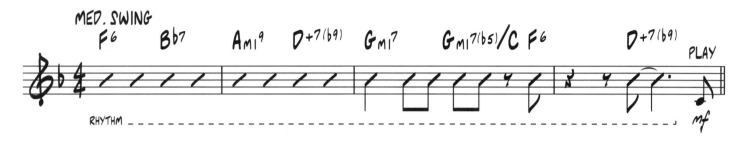

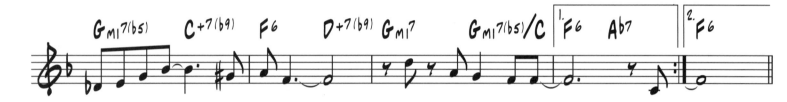

TO CODA ⊕

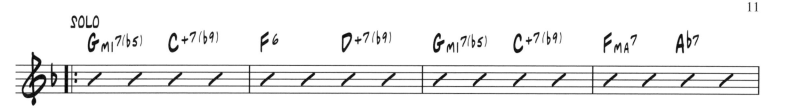

I AIN'T GOT NOTHIN' BUT THE BLUES

CD
13 : SPLIT TRACK/MELODY
14 : FULL STEREO TRACK

WORDS BY DON GEORGE
MUSIC BY DUKE ELLINGTON

C VERSION

MED. SWING

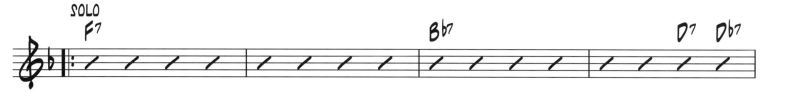

CD

15 : SPLIT TRACK/MELODY
16 : FULL STEREO TRACK

C VERSION

I DIDN'T KNOW ABOUT YOU

WORDS BY BOB RUSSELL
MUSIC BY DUKE ELLINGTON

SLOW SWING

15

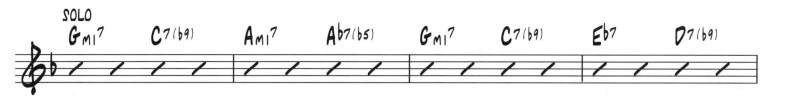

LOTUS BLOSSOM

MUSIC BY BILLY STRAYHORN

CD

17 : SPLIT TRACK/MELODY
18 : FULL STEREO TRACK

C VERSION

CD
19 : SPLIT TRACK/MELODY
20 : FULL STEREO TRACK

LOVE YOU MADLY

BY DUKE ELLINGTON

C VERSION

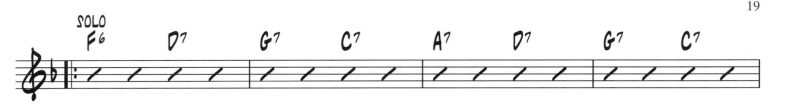

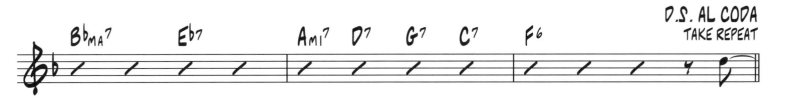

CD
1 : SPLIT TRACK/MELODY
2 : FULL STEREO TRACK

CHELSEA BRIDGE

BY BILLY STRAYHORN

Bb VERSION

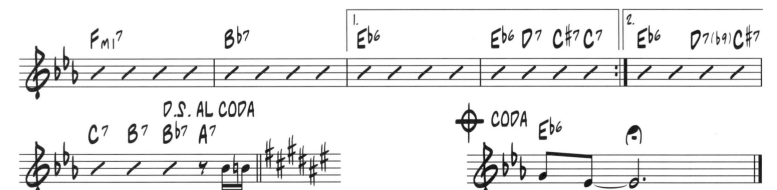

CD
3 : SPLIT TRACK/MELODY
4 : FULL STEREO TRACK

THE CREOLE LOVE CALL

BY DUKE ELLINGTON

Bb VERSION

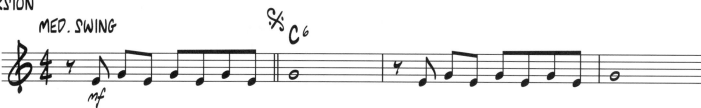

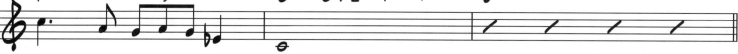

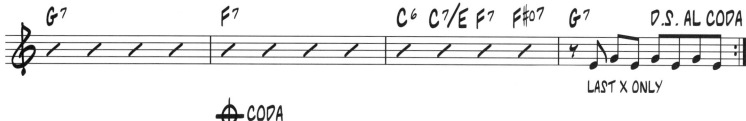

DANCERS IN LOVE

BY DUKE ELLINGTON

DAY DREAM

BY DUKE ELLINGTON AND
BILLY STRAYHORN

DROP ME OFF IN HARLEM

WORDS BY NICK KENNY
MUSIC BY DUKE ELLINGTON

EVERYTHING BUT YOU

BY DUKE ELLINGTON,
HARRY JAMES AND DON GEORGE

Bb VERSION

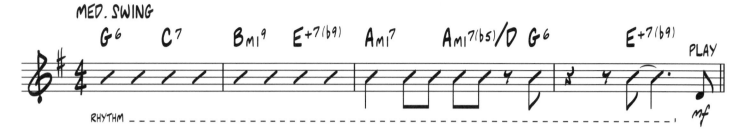

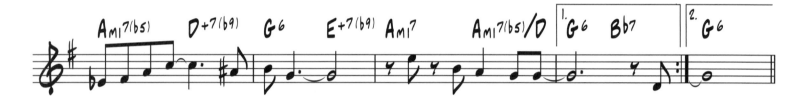

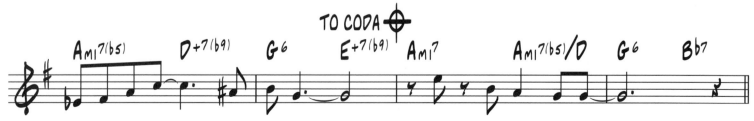

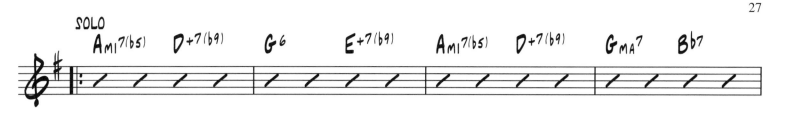

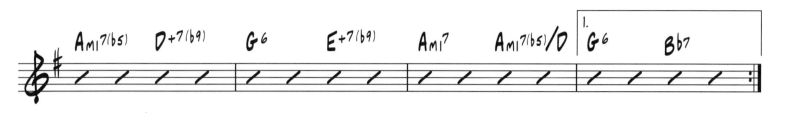

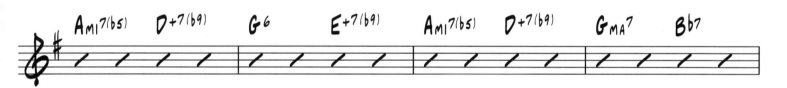

I AIN'T GOT NOTHIN' BUT THE BLUES

CD
13 : SPLIT TRACK/MELODY
14 : FULL STEREO TRACK

WORDS BY DON GEORGE
MUSIC BY DUKE ELLINGTON

Bb VERSION

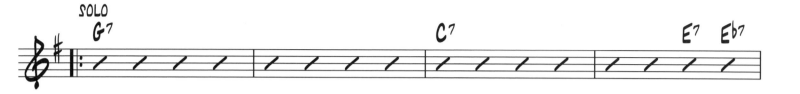

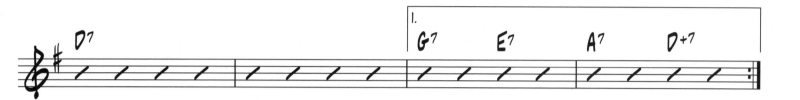

CD

15 : SPLIT TRACK/MELODY
16 : FULL STEREO TRACK

I DIDN'T KNOW ABOUT YOU

WORDS BY BOB RUSSELL
MUSIC BY DUKE ELLINGTON

Bb VERSION

SLOW SWING

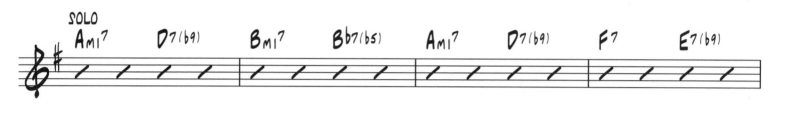

Lotus Blossom

CD
17: SPLIT TRACK/MELODY
18: FULL STEREO TRACK

MUSIC BY BILLY STRAYHORN

Bb VERSION

JAZZ WALTZ

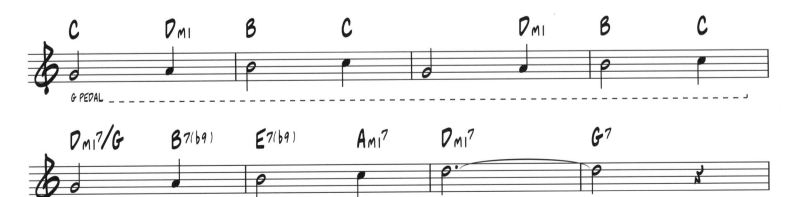

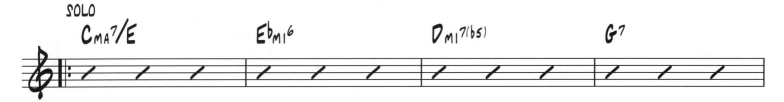

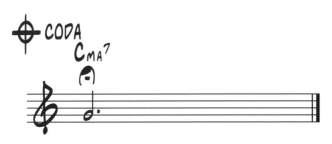

LOVE YOU MADLY

BY DUKE ELLINGTON

Bb VERSION

MED. SWING

TO CODA ⊕

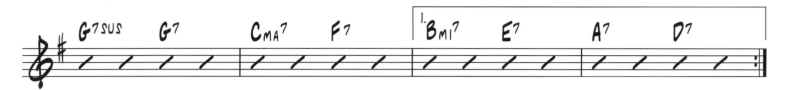

CHELSEA BRIDGE

BY BILLY STRAYHORN

CD
❸ : SPLIT TRACK/MELODY
❹ : FULL STEREO TRACK

THE CREOLE LOVE CALL

BY DUKE ELLINGTON

Eb VERSION

DANCERS IN LOVE

CD
- 5 : SPLIT TRACK/MELODY
- 6 : FULL STEREO TRACK

BY DUKE ELLINGTON

Eb VERSION   FAST SWING

CD
◆ 9 : SPLIT TRACK/MELODY
◆ 10 : FULL STEREO TRACK

DROP ME OFF IN HARLEM

WORDS BY NICK KENNY
MUSIC BY DUKE ELLINGTON

Eb VERSION

EVERYTHING BUT YOU

BY DUKE ELLINGTON,
HARRY JAMES AND DON GEORGE

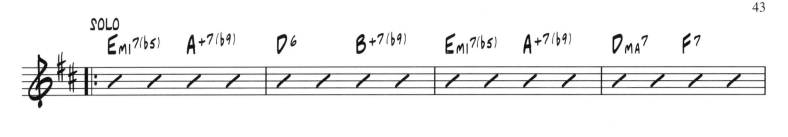

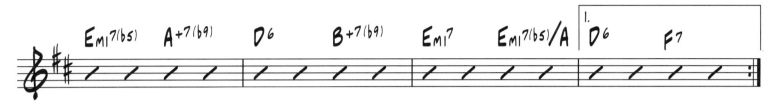

I AIN'T GOT NOTHIN' BUT THE BLUES

CD
13 : SPLIT TRACK/MELODY
14 : FULL STEREO TRACK

WORDS BY DON GEORGE
MUSIC BY DUKE ELLINGTON

Eb VERSION

MED. SWING

I DIDN'T KNOW ABOUT YOU

WORDS BY BOB RUSSELL
MUSIC BY DUKE ELLINGTON

CD

15 : SPLIT TRACK/MELODY
16 : FULL STEREO TRACK

Eb VERSION

SLOW SWING

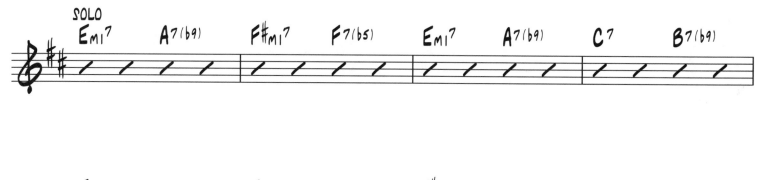

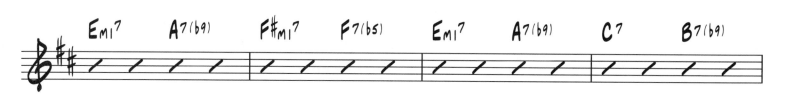

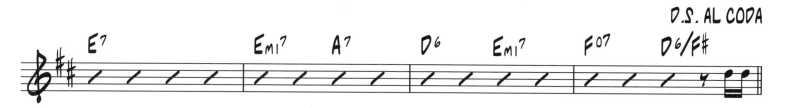

LOTUS BLOSSOM

MUSIC BY BILLY STRAYHORN

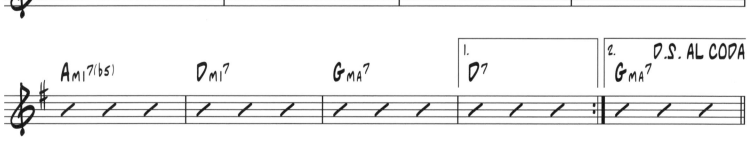

LOVE YOU MADLY

BY DUKE ELLINGTON

Eb VERSION

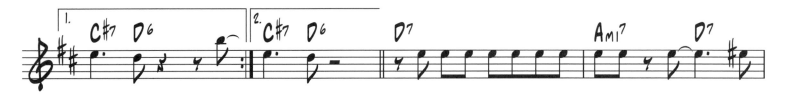

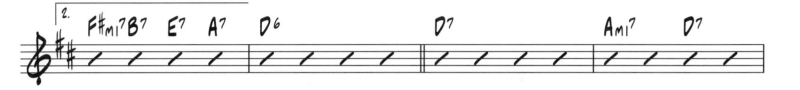

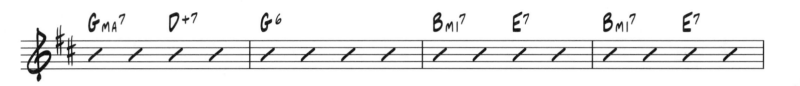

CHELSEA BRIDGE

BY BILLY STRAYHORN

CD
3 : SPLIT TRACK/MELODY
4 : FULL STEREO TRACK

THE CREOLE LOVE CALL

BY DUKE ELLINGTON

𝄢 : C VERSION

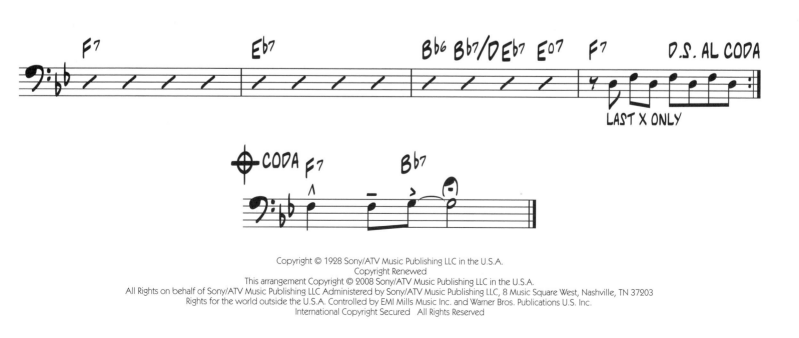

DANCERS IN LOVE

BY DUKE ELLINGTON

DAY DREAM

BY DUKE ELLINGTON AND
BILLY STRAYHORN

𝄢: C VERSION

DROP ME OFF IN HARLEM

WORDS BY NICK KENNY
MUSIC BY DUKE ELLINGTON

CD

11 : SPLIT TRACK/MELODY

12 : FULL STEREO TRACK

EVERYTHING BUT YOU

BY DUKE ELLINGTON,
HARRY JAMES AND DON GEORGE

𝄢: C VERSION

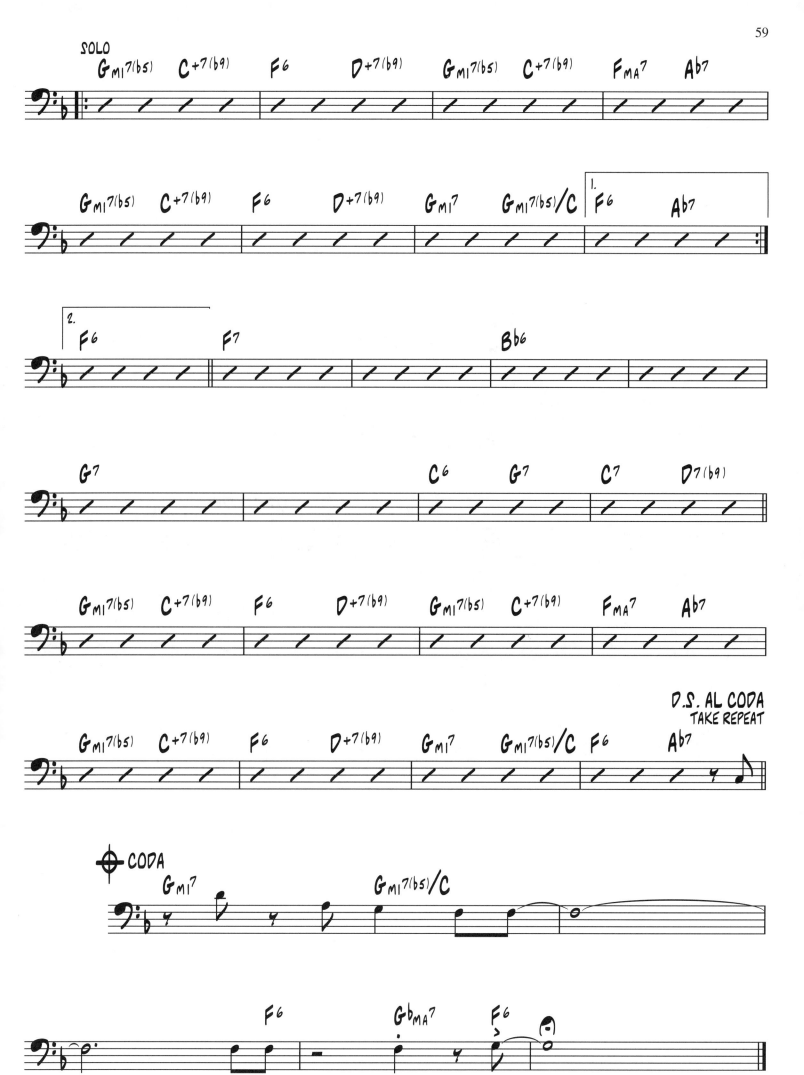

I AIN'T GOT NOTHIN' BUT THE BLUES

CD
13 : SPLIT TRACK/MELODY
14 : FULL STEREO TRACK

WORDS BY DON GEORGE
MUSIC BY DUKE ELLINGTON

♪: C VERSION

MED. SWING

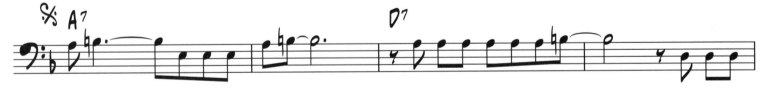

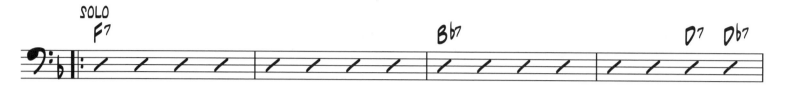

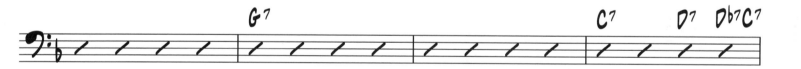

I Didn't Know About You

WORDS BY BOB RUSSELL
MUSIC BY DUKE ELLINGTON

CD
15 : SPLIT TRACK/MELODY
16 : FULL STEREO TRACK

𝄢: C VERSION

SLOW SWING

LOTUS BLOSSOM

MUSIC BY BILLY STRAYHORN

LOVE YOU MADLY

BY DUKE ELLINGTON

CD
19: SPLIT TRACK/MELODY
20: FULL STEREO TRACK

𝄢: C VERSION

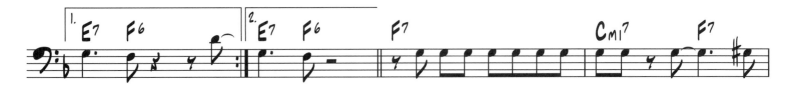

TO CODA ⊕

BOSSA NOVA Vol. 40
Black Orpheus • Call Me • A Man and a Woman • Only Trust Your Heart • The Shadow of Your Smile • Watch What Happens • Wave • and more.
00843036 ....$14.95

CLASSIC DUKE ELLINGTON Vol. 41
Cotton Tail • Do Nothin' Till You Hear from Me • I Got It Bad and That Ain't Good • I'm Beginning to See the Light • Mood Indigo • Solitude • and more.
00843037 ....$15.95

GERRY MULLIGAN FAVORITES Vol. 42
Bark for Barksdale • Dragonfly • Elevation • Idol Gossip • Jeru • The Lonely Night (Night Lights) • Noblesse • Rock Salt a/k/a Rocker • Theme for Jobim • Wallflower.
00843038 ....$15.95

GERRY MULLIGAN CLASSICS Vol. 43
Apple Core • Line for Lyons • Nights at the Turntable • Song for Strayhorn • Walkin' Shoes • and more.
00843039 ....$16.95

OLIVER NELSON Vol. 44
The Drive • Emancipation Blues • Hoe-Down • I Remember Bird • Miss Fine • Stolen Moments • Straight Ahead • Teenie's Blues • Yearnin'.
00843040 ....$16.95

JAZZ AT THE MOVIES Vol. 45
Baby Elephant Walk • God Bless' the Child • The Look of Love • The Rainbow Connection • Swinging on a Star • Thanks for the Memory • and more.
00843041 ....$14.95

BROADWAY JAZZ STANDARDS Vol. 46
Ain't Misbehavin' • I've Grown Accustomed to Her Face • Make Someone Happy • Old Devil Moon • Small World • Till There Was You • and more.
00843042 ....$14.95

CLASSIC JAZZ BALLADS Vol. 47
Blame It on My Youth • It's Easy to Remember • June in January • Love Letters • A Nightingale Sang in Berkeley Square • When I Fall in Love • and more.
00843043 ....$14.95

BEBOP CLASSICS Vol. 48
Be-Bop • Bird Feathers • Blue 'N Boogie • Byrd Like • Cool Blues • Dance of the Indifels • Dexterity • Dizzy Atmosphere • Groovin' High • Tempus Fugit.
00843044 ....$15.95

MILES DAVIS STANDARDS Vol. 49
Darn That Dream • I Loves You, Porgy • If I Were a Bell • On Green Dolphin Street • Some Day My Prince Will Come • Yesterdays • and more.
00843045 ....$16.95

GREAT JAZZ CLASSICS Vol. 50
Along Came Betty • Birdland • The Jive Samba • Little Sunflower • Nuages • Peri's Scope • Phase Dance • Road Song • Think on Me • Windows.
00843046 ....$14.95

UP-TEMPO JAZZ Vol. 51
Cherokee (Indian Love Song) • Chi Chi • 52nd Street Theme • Little Willie Leaps • Move • Pent Up House • Topsy • and more.
00843047 ....$14.95

STEVIE WONDER Vol. 52
I Just Called to Say I Love You • Isn't She Lovely • My Cherie Amour • Part Time Lover • Superstition • You Are the Sunshine of My Life • and more.
00843048 ....$15.95

RHYTHM CHANGES Vol. 53
Celia • Chasing the Bird • Cotton Tail • Crazeology • Fox Hunt • I Got Rhythm • No Moe • Oleo • Red Cross • Steeplechase.
00843049 ....$14.95

"MOONLIGHT IN VERMONT" AND OTHER GREAT STANDARDS Vol. 54
A Child Is Born • Love You Madly • Lover Man (Oh, Where Can You Be?) • Moonlight in Vermont • The Night Has a Thousand Eyes • Small Fry • and more.
00843050 ....$14.95

BENNY GOLSON Vol. 55
Along Came Betty • Blues March • Gypsy Jingle-Jangle • I Remember Clifford • Killer Joe • Step Lightly • Whisper Not • and more.
00843052 ....$15.95

VINCE GUARALDI Vol. 57
Blue Charlie Brown • Christmas Time Is Here • Frieda (With the Naturally Curly Hair) • The Great Pumpkin Waltz • Happiness Theme • Linus and Lucy • Oh, Good Grief • The Pebble Beach Theme • Skating • Surfin' Snoopy.
00843057 ....$15.95

MORE LENNON AND McCARTNEY Vol. 58
Can't Buy Me Love • Michelle • Norwegian Wood (This Bird Has Flown) • Eight Days a Week • Yellow Submarine • In My Life • The Long and Winding Road • All My Loving • Julia • Ob-La-Di, Ob-La-Da.
00843059 ....$14.95

SOUL JAZZ Vol. 59
The Cape Verdean Blues • Cold Duck Time • Dat Dere • Freight Trane • Holy Land • The Jive Samba • Nutville • Unit Seven • Work Song.
00843060 ....$14.95

MONGO SANTAMARIA Vol. 61
Afro Blue • Come Candellia • Federico • Las Guajiras • Linda Guajira • Manila • Sabroso • Watermelon Man.
00843062 ....$15.95

JAZZ-ROCK FUSION Vol. 62
Brown Hornet • Chameleon • Got a Match? • Loose Ends • Revelation • Snakes • Spain • Three Views of a Secret • Watermelon Man.
00843063 ....$14.95

CLASSICAL JAZZ Vol. 63
Eine Kleine Nachtmusik • Emperor Waltz • Habanera • Jesu, Joy of Man's Desiring • Minuet in G • New World Symphony (Theme) • Nocturne in F Minor • Ode to Joy • Pavane • Pavane (For a Dead Princess).
00843064 ....$14.95

TV TUNES Vol. 64
Bandstand Boogie • Theme from Family Guy • Theme from Frasier • Hawaii Five-O Theme • Love and Marriage • Mission: Impossible Theme • The Odd Couple • Theme from the Simpsons • Theme from Spider Man • Theme from Star Trek®.
00843065 ....$14.95

SMOOTH JAZZ Vol. 65
Angela • Cast Your Fate to the Wind • Feels So Good • Give Me the Night • Just the Two of Us • Minute by Minute • Morning Dance • Songbird • Street Life • This Masquerade.
00843066 ....$14.95

A CHARLIE BROWN CHRISTMAS Vol. 66
Christmas Is Coming • The Christmas Song (Chestnuts Roasting on an Open Fire) • Christmas Time Is Here • Linus and Lucy • My Little Drum • O Tannenbaum • Skating • What Child Is This.
00843067 ....$15.95

CHICK COREA Vol. 67
Bud Powell • Captain Marvel • 500 Miles High • Litha • The Loop • Mirror, Mirror • Now He Beats the Drum, Now He Stops • (I Can Recall) Spain • Tones for Joan's Bones • Windows.
00843068 ....$15.95

CHARLES MINGUS Vol. 68
Better Get Hit in Your Soul • Boogie Stop Shuffle • Goodbye Pork Pie Hat • Gunslinging Bird • Jelly Roll • Nostalgia in Times Square • Peggy's Blue Skylight • Pithecanthropus Erectus • Portrait • Slippers.
00843069 ....$16.95

CLASSIC JAZZ Vol. 69
Allen's Alley • Detour Ahead • I Wished on the Moon • Let's Get Lost • Nobody Else but Me • Our Delight • Rockin' in Rhythm • A Sleepin' Bee • Soul Eyes • What Is There to Say.
00843071 ....$14.95

THE DOORS Vol. 70
Break on Through to the Other Side • The End • Hello, I Love You (Won't You Tell Me Your Name?) • L.A. Woman • Light My Fire • Love Me Two Times • People Are Strange • Riders on the Storm • Roadhouse Blues • Touch Me.
00843072 ....$14.95

COLE PORTER CLASSICS Vol. 71
Dream Dancing • From This Moment On • I Get a Kick out of You • I Love Paris • I've Got My Eyes on You • Just One of Those Things • Love for Sale • My Heart Belongs to Daddy • Night and Day • What Is This Thing Called Love?
00843073 ....$14.95

CLASSIC JAZZ BALLADS Vol. 72
For Heaven's Sake • Isfahan • Lament • Maybe You'll Be There • The Single Petal of a Rose • Some Other Spring • Sure Thing • Too Young to Go Steady • You're Looking at Me • You've Changed.
00843074 ....$14.95

JAZZ/BLUES Vol. 73
Break Out the Blues • Bremond's Blues • Gee Baby, Ain't I Good to You • I'll Close My Eyes • Movin' Along (Sid's Twelve) • Night Lights • Reunion Blues • The Sermon • Sunny • This Here.
00843075 ....$14.95

0108

ARTIST TRANSCRIPTIONS

Artist Transcriptions are authentic, note-for-note transcriptions of today's hottest artists in jazz, pop and rock. These outstanding, accurate arrangements are in an easy-to-read format which includes all essential lines. Artist Transcriptions can be used to perform, sequence or for reference.

CLARINET

00672423	Buddy De Franco Collection	$19.95

FLUTE

00672379	Eric Dolphy Collection	$19.95
00672372	James Moody Collection – Sax and Flute	$19.95
00660108	James Newton – Improvising Flute	$14.95
00672455	Lew Tabackin Collection	$19.95

GUITAR & BASS

00660113	The Guitar Style of George Benson	$14.95
00672331	Ron Carter – Acoustic Bass	$16.95
00660115	Al Di Meola – Friday Night in San Francisco	$14.95
00604043	Al Di Meola – Music, Words, Pictures	$14.95
00673245	Jazz Style of Tal Farlow	$19.95
00672359	Bela Fleck and the Flecktones	$18.95
00699389	Jim Hall – Jazz Guitar Environments	$19.95
00699306	Jim Hall – Exploring Jazz Guitar	$19.95
00672335	Best of Scott Henderson	$24.95
00672356	Jazz Guitar Standards	$19.95
00675536	Wes Montgomery – Guitar Transcriptions	$17.95
00672353	Joe Pass Collection	$18.95
00673216	John Patitucci	$16.95
00672374	Johnny Smith Guitar Solos	$16.95
00672320	Mark Whitfield	$19.95
00672337	Gary Willis Collection	$19.95

PIANO & KEYBOARD

00672338	Monty Alexander Collection	$19.95
00672487	Monty Alexander Plays Standards	$19.95
00672318	Kenny Barron Collection	$22.95
00672520	Count Basie Collection	$19.95
00672364	Warren Bernhardt Collection	$19.95
00672439	Cyrus Chestnut Collection	$19.95
00673242	Billy Childs Collection	$19.95
00672300	Chick Corea – Paint the World	$12.95
00672537	Bill Evans at Town Hall	$16.95
00672425	Bill Evans – Piano Interpretations	$19.95
00672365	Bill Evans – Piano Standards	$19.95
00672510	Bill Evans Trio – Vol. 1: 1959-1961	$24.95
00672511	Bill Evans Trio – Vol. 2: 1962-1965	$24.95
00672512	Bill Evans Trio – Vol. 3: 1968-1974	$24.95
00672513	Bill Evans Trio – Vol. 4: 1979-1980	$24.95
00672329	Benny Green Collection	$19.95
00672486	Vince Guaraldi Collection	$19.95
00672419	Herbie Hancock Collection	$19.95
00672446	Gene Harris Collection	$19.95
00672438	Hampton Hawes	$19.95
00672322	Ahmad Jamal Collection	$22.95
00672476	Brad Mehldau Collection	$19.95

00672390	Thelonious Monk Plays Jazz Standards – Volume 1	$19.95
00672391	Thelonious Monk Plays Jazz Standards – Volume 2	$19.95
00672433	Jelly Roll Morton – The Piano Rolls	$12.95
00672542	Oscar Peterson – Jazz Piano Solos	$14.95
00672544	Oscar Peterson – Originals	$9.95
00672532	Oscar Peterson – Plays Broadway	$19.95
00672531	Oscar Peterson – Plays Duke Ellington	$19.95
00672533	Oscar Peterson – Trios	$24.95
00672543	Oscar Peterson Trio – Canadiana Suite	$7.95
00672534	Very Best of Oscar Peterson	$22.95
00672371	Bud Powell Classics	$19.95
00672376	Bud Powell Collection	$19.95
00672437	André Previn Collection	$19.95
00672507	Gonzalo Rubalcaba Collection	$19.95
00672303	Horace Silver Collection	$19.95
00672316	Art Tatum Collection	$22.95
00672355	Art Tatum Solo Book	$19.95
00672357	Billy Taylor Collection	$24.95
00673215	McCoy Tyner	$16.95
00672321	Cedar Walton Collection	$19.95
00672519	Kenny Werner Collection	$19.95
00672434	Teddy Wilson Collection	$19.95

SAXOPHONE

00673244	Julian "Cannonball" Adderley Collection	$19.95
00673237	Michael Brecker	$19.95
00672429	Michael Brecker Collection	$19.95
00672351	Brecker Brothers... And All Their Jazz	$19.95
00672447	Best of the Brecker Brothers	$19.95
00672315	Benny Carter Plays Standards	$22.95
00672314	Benny Carter Collection	$22.95
00672394	James Carter Collection	$19.95
00672349	John Coltrane Plays Giant Steps	$19.95
00672529	John Coltrane – Giant Steps	$14.95
00672494	John Coltrane – A Love Supreme	$14.95
00672493	John Coltrane Plays "Coltrane Changes"	$19.95
00672453	John Coltrane Plays Standards	$19.95
00673233	John Coltrane Solos	$22.95
00672328	Paul Desmond Collection	$19.95
00672454	Paul Desmond – Standard Time	$19.95
00672379	Eric Dolphy Collection	$19.95
00672530	Kenny Garrett Collection	$19.95
00699375	Stan Getz	$18.95
00672377	Stan Getz – Bossa Novas	$19.95
00672375	Stan Getz – Standards	$17.95
00673254	Great Tenor Sax Solos	$18.95
00672523	Coleman Hawkins Collection	$19.95
00673252	Joe Henderson – Selections from "Lush Life" & "So Near So Far"	$19.95
00672330	Best of Joe Henderson	$22.95

00673239	Best of Kenny G	$19.95
00673229	Kenny G – Breathless	$19.95
00672462	Kenny G – Classics in the Key of G	$19.95
00672485	Kenny G – Faith: A Holiday Album	$14.95
00672373	Kenny G – The Moment	$19.95
00672516	Kenny G – Paradise	$14.95
00672326	Joe Lovano Collection	$19.95
00672498	Jackie McLean Collection	$19.95
00672372	James Moody Collection – Sax and Flute	$19.95
00672416	Frank Morgan Collection	$19.95
00672539	Gerry Mulligan Collection	$19.95
00672352	Charlie Parker Collection	$19.95
00672444	Sonny Rollins Collection	$19.95
00675000	David Sanborn Collection	$16.95
00672528	Bud Shank Collection	$19.95
00672491	New Best of Wayne Shorter	$19.95
00672455	Lew Tabackin Collection	$19.95
00672334	Stanley Turrentine Collection	$19.95
00672524	Lester Young Collection	$19.95

TROMBONE

00672332	J.J. Johnson Collection	$19.95
00672489	Steve Turré Collection	$19.95

TRUMPET

00672480	Louis Armstrong Collection	$14.95
00672481	Louis Armstrong Plays Standards	$14.95
00672435	Chet Baker Collection	$19.95
00673234	Randy Brecker	$17.95
00672351	Brecker Brothers... And All Their Jazz	$19.95
00672447	Best of the Brecker Brothers	$19.95
00672448	Miles Davis – Originals, Vol. 1	$19.95
00672451	Miles Davis – Originals, Vol. 2	$19.95
00672450	Miles Davis – Standards, Vol. 1	$19.95
00672449	Miles Davis – Standards, Vol. 2	$19.95
00672479	Dizzy Gillespie Collection	$19.95
00673214	Freddie Hubbard	$14.95
00672382	Tom Harrell – Jazz Trumpet	$19.95
00672363	Jazz Trumpet Solos	$9.95
00672506	Chuck Mangione Collection	$19.95
00672525	Arturo Sandoval – Trumpet Evolution	$19.95

THE BIG BAND PLAY-ALONG SERIES

These revolutionary play-along packs are great products for those who want a big band sound to back up their instrument, without the pressure of playing solo. They're perfect for current players and for those former players who want to get back in the swing!

Each volume includes:

- Easy-to-read, authentic big band arrangements
- Professional recordings on CD of all the big band instruments, including the lead part
- Editions for alto sax, tenor sax, trumpet, trombone, guitar, piano, bass, and drums

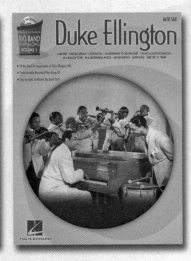

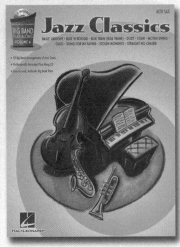

1. SWING FAVORITES

April in Paris • I've Got You Under My Skin • In the Mood • It Don't Mean a Thing (If It Ain't Got That Swing) • Route 66 • Speak Low • Stompin' at the Savoy • Tangerine • This Can't Be Love • Until I Met You (Corner Pocket).

07011313	Alto Sax	$14.95
07011314	Tenor Sax	$14.95
07011315	Trumpet	$14.95
07011316	Trombone	$14.95
07011317	Guitar	$14.95
07011318	Piano	$14.95
07011319	Bass	$14.95
07011320	Drums	$14.95

2. POPULAR HITS

Ain't No Mountain High Enough • Brick House • Copacabana (At the Copa) • Evil Ways • I Heard It Through the Grapevine • On Broadway • Respect • Street Life • Yesterday • Zoot Suit Riot.

07011321	Alto Sax	$14.95
07011322	Tenor Sax	$14.95
07011323	Trumpet	$14.95
07011324	Trombone	$14.95
07011325	Guitar	$14.95
07011326	Piano	$14.95
07011327	Bass	$14.95
07011328	Drums	$14.95

3. DUKE ELLINGTON

Caravan • Chelsea Bridge • Cotton Tail • I'm Beginning to See the Light • I'm Just a Lucky So and So • In a Mellow Tone • In a Sentimental Mood • Mood Indigo • Satin Doll • Take the "A" Train.

00843086	Alto Sax	$14.95
00843087	Tenor Sax	$14.95
00843088	Trumpet	$14.95
00843089	Trombone	$14.95
00843090	Guitar	$14.95
00843091	Piano	$14.95
00843092	Bass	$14.95
00843093	Drums	$14.95

4. JAZZ CLASSICS

Bags' Groove • Blue 'N Boogie • Blue Train (Blue Trane) • Doxy • Four • Moten Swing • Oleo • Song for My Father • Stolen Moments • Straight No Chaser.

00843094	Alto Sax	$14.95
00843095	Tenor Sax	$14.95
00843096	Trumpet	$14.95
00843097	Trombone	$14.95
00843098	Guitar	$14.95
00843099	Piano	$14.95
00843100	Bass	$14.95
00843101	Drums	$14.95

HAL•LEONARD® CORPORATION

7777 W. BLUEMOUND RD. P.O. BOX 13819 MILWAUKEE, WI 53213

Prices, contents and availability subject to change without notice.